"I want to give this book to every person I have ever counsele with your child lovingly is so radical and so sweet, and so nec addresses the realities, needs, and logistics of parenting and h in order to be the parent you want to be. It's full of sweet moments, good ideas, and helpful prompts to get you away from desperation, panic, or punishment, and back onto the same team as your child. This is a radically different and sweet approach and I am bursting with ideas on how to use it in my practice."

-Roya Dedeaux, M.S, MFTI

"Flo's process is simple, and challenging, deep and personal in the way this kind of work must be if we wish to truly have the breakthroughs (versus breakdowns) we need to have as parents. At the same time she's done what is so difficult to do: taken a very emotionally charged and overwhelming process and cut through all the complexity in order to give us a practice we can implement both in and outside of those big parenting moments.

We have the choice whether to spend our energy trying to breathe beneath the mess we're burying ourselves under, or the powerful work that Flo is offering that will dig us back out again. I have no doubt that this book will change the lives of those who truly dig into it."

-Tara Wagner,   life coach and creator of the Digging Deep process and the Organic Sisterhood

"This is an amazing book that every parent should read. I feel inspired to not settle for being a good-enough parent, but to become the best parent I can be to my kids. The Action Ideas will help me get there!"

-Angela L., mother of three

"I found the parenting suggestions made in Keep Your Cool practical and very positive. I happen to be reading another parenting book at the same time and while useful, it was a little dry and matter-of-fact. Keep Your Cool is uplifting and every time I picked it up I left feeling lively, confident and ready to connect with my children. I appreciate the examples given based on the author's personal experience. This book has very thoughtful and helpful tips."

-Gardenia Gomez, mother of two

Keep Your Cool

How to Stop Yelling, Spanking & Punishing:

What To Do Instead

———————————————————

Keep Your Cool

How to Stop Yelling, Spanking & Punishing:

What To Do Instead

Flo Gascon

Published in the United States by Shady Grove Media, San Marcos, CA.

ISBN: 978-0615891330

First Edition 2013

www.flogascon.com

Dedicated to my boundless girl with curly hair and her compassionate sister with love to spare.

Together we offer this book in honor of a baby girl named Daisy and her inspiring mother.

May we all touch our precious children with love and kindness each day we are fortunate to have them.

Table of Contents

How to Use this Guide

1. Devote some dedicated time to this work. Prepare yourself to be open, curious, nonjudgmental and present. Deep honesty in your answers is necessary. Breathe through any sadness, guilt, shame or anger that may arise. Let them go so you can move forward.

2. Work through one section/step at a time, answering the questions fully. You may skip around to make this process work for you but I do recommend completing a section before moving on.

3. Choose your favorite action ideas and use them. Add your own.

4. When you have worked through the entire guide, copy your Quick Start and keep it available as a summary. Then go hug your kids and tell them you love them, just for good measure. You all can never have too much love.

5. Implement and review as necessary. As things change, adjust.

Everything contained in this guide assumes a safe environment and that no one is in danger.

If there is an imminent threat, intervene immediately - don't stop to breathe or think about the best approach.

After you have scooped your child up, stopped the hand ready to hit or throw something, moved to safer ground, etc, *then* take a deep breath and continue this process. Safety first.

Introduction: My Story

I was a wonderful parent for many years. Our home was peaceful, my daughters were content and easy-going, I was calm and gentle. Although I was often tired, life was wonderful and I thought I had everything figured out. We had always been an attachment parenting family - it was easy and natural for me and fell in line with the loving, aware style I wanted.

When my youngest child was about two years old, I entered a new phase of my parenting journey. For no apparent reason, my daughter was becoming upset very often and nothing I could do helped. In fact, I often made things worse with my inability to stay calm and think in the heat of the moment. I felt like an utter failure.

For a couple of years I worked with my little girl to help her with her emotions, to help her learn how to settle into this big world we shared. My own deep emotions were triggered causing me to lose my temper again and again. All of my attentive communication skills were buried in overwhelm. It was a difficult time, but it was also a time of great learning and love. When I was in the midst of it, I couldn't see that our struggles were such a tiny part of our time together. Mostly, we were happy and had a wonderful relationship. And in fact, she was giving me signals all the time of just how much she trusted and connected to me. But those challenging moments felt so big that it was easy for me to blow it out of proportion. I lost objectivity. I lost patience. I lost myself.

I remember sitting at a friend's kitchen table. My daughter had just scampered off after I soothed her for what seemed like an hour. My friend said to me, "You are such a great mother," and I burst into tears. I couldn't see it. All I could see was the way I raised my voice more often than I wanted to. The way I scared even myself with my anger and frustration. I allowed my emotions to take control in those moments. Even though I never punished, ignored or gave up on my daughter, I thought the worst of myself. I knew I could do better. My daughter needed me to be my best self.

I knew that every time I reacted badly, I was damaging our relationship. How I handled all of those little moments had big implications. If I wanted my daughter to trust me and talk to me, it was important to create a positive intimacy, not one full of negative consequences. I wanted to get back to being the mother I was before I was overwhelmed - the one who responded with listening and flexibility.

Happily, I figured it out. I learned how to handle the heat of the moment without yelling, spanking or punishing. It's been years since I felt so lost, and my relationship with both of my children is beautifully intact. The secret to my success? It's in these pages. I did the work. I asked myself some deep, difficult questions. I learned a lot about myself and re-affirmed what I wanted to accomplish as a mother. I committed to my parenting style, to my child and to our relationship. I gained valuable skills that I use in *all* of my relationships, including the one with myself. I slowed down and developed specific ways that I could navigate challenging moments. Whether it is a troublesome behavior, an argument with a sibling, a heartbreaking disappointment, an inability to understand, a difference of opinion, a break-down in communication, conflicting needs or desires or whatever scenario arises, I can handle it with grace, gentleness, patience and calm. No more yelling and anger.

I know I am not alone. We all want to be kind and loving parents. I am giving you the handy bag of tricks I wish I had had. It is my great hope that you take my techniques, put them into action, do the inner examination, and get back to enjoying your child.

The relationship you have with your son or daughter is the foundation for everything. Build with love, don't tear down with fear. Connect, don't withdraw. Listen, don't shush. Ask, don't tell. Hold, don't banish.

Why Is It So Hard?

No one wants to be harsh with their children. Yet, this is one of the most common struggles parents encounter and one of the most difficult to overcome. As babies become toddlers and beyond, the tender, loving care we offered so instinctively gets lost as we expect more and more.

Our own self-care isn't adequate.
When we aren't physically feeling our best, we don't have stamina from which to draw. In a word, we're overwhelmed.

Our plates get fuller.
As our little ones need us a little less, we try to do more. It's easy to over-extend ourselves.

Our family grows.
We may add more children or pets or welcome parents to live with us as they age. More personalities and needs equals more to consider.

Our support networks don't exist.
Gone are the days of extended family and friends who regularly pitched in to help. We do it all ourselves.

Our time is in short supply.
Many households have both parents working outside the home in addition to kids' activities and general life maintenance. We're too busy to pay attention.

Our ideals are unrealistic.
We are unwilling to change our course when our kids don't or can't follow our expectations. Tensions rise and create power struggles.

Our concerns in the past/our thoughts for the future cloud judgment.
It becomes challenging to remain aware of and centered in the present moment. We react quickly rather than respond intelligently.

The Heat of the Moment

When we're tired, busy, stressed or in the middle of something, we can be quick to snap. Personalities clash. Being caught off guard can send us spinning out of control. We may not even recognize ourselves when we lose it. We may think we're being observed and judged by others.

When your daughter is melting down in the grocery store you fear the disapproving looks and judgement on your sweet girl and you.

When your son isn't ready to get out of the pool yet, you're worried everyone is assessing your parenting skills and tsk-tsking you for raising someone who doesn't respect authority.

Being interrupted when we're just trying to finish this one last thing can easily push us over the edge. Your daughter is late and you've been worried about where she was. You just cleaned the house and it's a mess again. Or how about when you're experiencing doubt and your confidence is wavering? Any action that appears to validate your concern can send you tumbling into fear and feeling out of control. You can easily feel like you don't know what you are doing. Just when everything feels like the last straw, you begin grasping for them.

It can be intense. Our triggers run deep yet can crash through the surface quickly. When that moment arrives, whatever sparks it, you have choices to make. Your irritability, emotions, fear, concern, doubt, fatigue, familiar patterns rise up. Your chest might tighten, your heart races, angry words tumble through your mind or go straight to the tip of your tongue. Your fists might clench or your hand raise. You are about to react. Can you stop yourself from doing something that you'll wish you didn't do?

Does this sound familiar? Yes, our kids have triggers and big emotions, too. You've seen this same response in them. This is a place from which you can relate and find common ground. No one likes to feel this way and it can be confusing. Understand yourself and your child so you can chart a course through difficult times. Know how you can help and how to handle yourself when you can't.

We say and do things we don't want to, that we don't mean. It's unfortunate that we snap, yell, threaten, slam things, cause tears, take belongings and plans away, ground, punish, issue time-outs, raise our hands in anger and frustration. Common arguments occur over bedtimes, body care, clothing, meals, "getting along," ownership and care of belongings, homework, being dishonest, not following rules, name-calling, "not listening," and "being disrespectful." It moves beyond unfortunate and into harmful if you are parenting this way more often than not. It doesn't have to be this way.

> Yelling, punishing or spanking has no place in a respectful relationship, regardless of the ages. Help your child learn that by modeling it. Especially as they get older, you've got to walk the walk.

Wouldn't you rather have helpful conversations, the ability to see other points of view, patience, smiles, laughter, inside jokes, fun family outings, give and take, negotiation, connection, the opportunity to watch your kids blossom as they think for themselves? If you can have some other ideas ready you can change your course. You don't have to have regrets or make things worse.

Losing Your Temper Doesn't Work

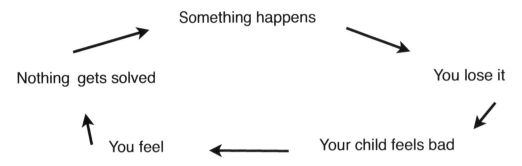

When you blow up, your focus shifts from what happened to crisis mode. We decide to fight by arguing or flee by punishing. What happened to the original problem? It got buried in the mess and will only re-surface again, perhaps bigger. Your child isn't learning how to solve problems, only how to survive them. Losing your temper demonstrates that losing control of your emotions is how to handle situations. So, how do you think they're going to handle situations?

The muscles you use get stronger. If you fight, you'll get better at arguing. If your child finds ways around punishment, she'll get better at finding ways around punishment (such as lying or being sneaky). If you want to play tug of war with your child, some day you're going to lose. You're bigger and stronger at first. The more you pull, the more your child pulls. All of this resistance is making your chid stronger at resisting you. The more you do this, the stronger those muscles get until they're better at it than you are. A child will get his needs met, with or without you. If you don't drop the rope and listen he will beat you at your own game.

Don't go for the easy out of using your power to create a struggle. It's not lasting and you will run out of options. Flex your problem-solving muscles instead and be inspired by what your child can do with those.

What You Can Do:
Release and Open to Love.

We can find ourselves head-to-head with our children. Individuals have differing points of view, ideas, desires, personalities, plans, expectations, goals, abilities, preferences and timelines. With all of that going on we're going to disagree sometimes. But it doesn't have to be a screaming match or a power struggle. We can handle situations with a calm demeanor and have peaceful resolution. As parents, we are in a position to model honorable behavior and problem solving skills. If we want our kids to develop listening skills, negotiation and critical thinking, conflict provides the perfect opportunity to practice. If we shut them down with a punishment or an order to be quiet, we're robbing everyone of an opportunity for connection and learning, including ourselves.

A word about punishment

Can you cut your kid some slack? Please consider the true lesson behind the punishment you dole out. How does being in a time-out help a young child learn not to hit his sister? It only serves to make him feel angry, helpless and alone. How does taking a phone away from an older child help them remember to come home on time? Maybe they need to set a timer on it to remind them because they are very impulsive and focused on their fun. Punishment doesn't get you anywhere productive or constructive or communicative. Build your relationship with this guide instead.

Giving children room to experiment with their growing minds and bodies is critical.

As they begin to make friendships and find their place in the world, they will meet a variety of circumstances, all of which offer many options.

They will have their own ideas. You will have disagreements. This is a time to work together not against each other.

Honor their individuality by recognizing it and not punishing them for it. Don't they deserve that much? Commit to taking responsibility for yourself while you guide your child with sensitivity as he or she slowly learns to take his or her own. It's a process that does not happen overnight. Rushing it will only set you all back.

We can't force an outcome or control the way people behave, but we can decide how we will approach situations. We can decide what kind of mom we want to be; how we want to build our relationship with our kids; and what they will be learning about problem solving, conflict resolution and positive communication. As parents we wield great influence. Let's make sure that it's a positive, nourishing one.

It doesn't mean that you are failing if you are struggling. It just means that every child is different and you have to open yourself a little wider. This isn't a time to quit or give up or accept a hardship. It certainly isn't a time to be harder on your child or tighten your control of them. It's time to admit that you need two things:

1. Time
2. New approaches

As hard as it can be, occasionally all you can do is wait. Growth happens. Bodies and brains change, life experiences shape our understanding, maturity moves things along. Nothing you do can make that process faster. Have patience and know that time itself will smooth many bumps. While you are waiting you can build your relationship rather than damage it. And what time can't help, you can by integrating some new thoughts and actions.

Roll up your Sleeves:
Reflect and Get into Action

Most of what you will read here is related to you. As the adult, it's your responsibility to control *your* impulses and know your priorities. Respect your child for the person that he or she is and give them the same attention that you would give anyone who needed help, had a request or made a mistake. If you can see children as people who can't quite say what they mean or understand the situation fully, people who are trying to be part of your world, people who want to be seen and heard and feel important, you will feel more approachable and willing to see through their eyes. They are people who don't know what to do with these big feelings - feelings that are bigger than themselves. They need someone bigger to help them through it. As they get older, they can feel very small as they begin to understand the complexity of their world.

When you can use their perspective, suddenly it's not a big, tangly mess but just something to work out.

That doesn't mean it's always straight-forward or quick. You can't make another cookie appear when you don't have any more flour and you can't play the DVD again when it's broken. Replacing a lost phone is costly. Sometimes the solution is delayed and that can be hard for your child. Sometimes there simply is no solution because there is no concrete problem or desire. Emotions may just be bubbling up that need releasing. `

What do you do when you don't know what else to do?

Have a Toolkit You Can Reach Into When the Moment Strikes

Be ready with your own best ideas. Have your priorities and what you know about you and your kids in the top of your mind, easily accessible when you need help to stay calm.

It's hard to make good decisions in the heat of the moment. It's difficult to keep our own emotions in check when those around you are escalating out of control. What if you could be ready? Not on guard or walking on eggshells but truly equipped if a conflict arises.

If you know ahead of time how to handle yourself, what causes an issue, what techniques work, what your goals are and where accountability lies, then you can confidently navigate the situation. Knowledge and preparation is powerful. Being clear in your intentions upfront is critically important because it's difficult to think when you are caught off-guard.

Taking some time to assess the skills, personalities and needs of your family members will go a long way in shortening the time it takes to defuse a situation. Or even prevent one in the first place.

Taking some time afterwards to process the experience gives valuable insights into how to adjust your approach. It also gives you an opportunity to reflect, release and admire (or forgive) your response. This builds your confidence and refreshes you.

This guide is meant to outline manageable steps to handling difficult moments peacefully.

It provides tips and tricks you can use to keep your cool and not damage your relationship with your kids. Each section has been designed to give you practical ideas you can implement immediately, doable actions for those times when you need to act before it gets worse.

You'll also find in-depth challenges and exercises to help you find lasting peace through improved communication and understanding. Do the work and dedicate yourself to the process of patience, examination and change.

Step 1: Stop Before You Start

Step 2: Identify the Problem

Step 3: Identify Accountability

Step 4: Identify Your Direction

Step 5: Conduct a Review

The process is not necessarily linear, with the exception of the first and last steps. With some experience you may be able to skip some steps altogether. Using them all, though, gives you a very clear picture of what you're dealing with and sets you up for a successful experience and positive resolution.

In the end you may find that you aren't really changing, just recovering your true self that's been buried in the mess and stress of a busy life.

Keep this in mind: Sometimes you aren't going to get your way.

Sometimes things won't be the way you want them to be. Sometimes things just happen. It goes south and you don't know why; you can't rescue it. This may be because you are dealing with a factor that is completely out of your control: biology.

°You simply cannot get a brain to reason when it's not wired to do so.

°You simply cannot force a body to sit still before it knows how to regulate its signals.

°You simply cannot advance to the next developmental stage until the mind and body are ready.

You just can't.

In those times, you will be frustrated. You will think it will never end. You will think that you have to be tough or else. You will think it is bigger than it is. You will be desperate and ready to try things you vowed you'd never do. You will revert to patterns and techniques that scared you as a child. You'll exhaust yourself with the worry that you aren't doing enough, that you are a bad parent.

I've been there. Time passes and with compassion and a supportive space, things change.

You can make things much worse in your struggle to control what you can't or what is another person's right to decide.

With patience and the love you have for the child you always vowed to protect, you can come out the other side with a trusting, strong relationship. Isn't that what we all want?

If you can find the positive qualities amid the hard bits, you will all benefit. When I moved from seeing my daughter as stubborn to determined, it shifted.

When you can't change something, you *can* see it differently. A positive perspective finds possibilities where a negative one throws the hands up in defeat.

- Move from bratty to confident.

- Move from whiny to expressive.

- Move from difficult to deep.

- Move from emotional to open.

- Move from trouble-maker to someone who is still learning.

- Move from problem child to your sweet baby.

A compassionate eye makes room for grace.

Take your open heart with you and be ready for a fresh approach to conflict. Work through the following chapters without judgement. Use the prompts to develop a strategy from conscious choice. Let go of any negativity you may harbor for your parenting journey thus far. This is not a time to be harsh with yourself for past actions - that doesn't help you move forward. Berating yourself keeps you stuck in negative behavior because you convince yourself that you can't do better. Yes, you can, and it begins with these small steps.

What to do instead of yelling, spanking or punishing when you don't know what else to do?

Let's explore a foundation with five universal principles.

Universal Principle 1

Let Go of What's Happening or Fear of the Future

We've taken on a lot as parents. It can be so scary to feel responsible for this life we've been entrusted with and we wrap ourselves in worry over our performance. Are we doing enough or too much? Am I preparing him properly for a secure, successful adulthood? How can I make sure she doesn't get into trouble and make life-altering mistakes? What can I do to make sure she is a productive member of society? If I don't get this under control now, what's going to happen? I need to get her to not behave that way or she'll never get anywhere. If he doesn't learn how to focus and work hard, he'll always struggle. We have such deep concern and love for our kids. We have so many insecurities about the future and we are so certain we know what's best. We've been there, right? Maybe. But what if all of that fear and preconceived notion is getting in the way of our ability to interact with the moment in which we are standing? Is it possible that we are manipulating the present with an unpredictable future? Our inability to know what will happen drives our attempts to bend future events to our will.

It's not wrong to look ahead. Knowing your destination is very useful and helps you know what steps you need to take to get there. However, trying to control the future is another concept entirely. There are twists and turns around every corner and considering that your child's life is not even yours, it's going to go places you can't predict. Ultimately we know this and the anxiety it causes motivates us to do all we can while we still have the opportunity. Unfortunately, it creates a snowball effect and before we know it we can lose touch with reality. We begin to invent scenarios and what-ifs that clearly demand we do even more to ensure they never happen. Our well-intentioned efforts can morph into unnecessary harmful control. Happily, most of our fears are never realized, so know that you can let them go without any unfortunate effects.

If you want to work through difficult situations with your child or avoid them altogether, let go of your fear of what is happening. Try to stay in tune with what you are actually seeing and hearing. Don't project your ideas of what this may lead to. Just let it be what it is right now. Don't give it any more power than that. If your child refuses to brush her teeth, acknowledge that she just doesn't want to brush her teeth *right now*. It doesn't mean she never will and her teeth will fall out. It doesn't mean that she won't ever listen to you. It doesn't mean that she is testing your limits. It might mean that her teeth are sensitive right now or she doesn't like that toothpaste or she's too tired. It might mean a lot but all you know for sure is that she doesn't want to right now. Keep your fear and your stories and your own experiences out of it because you are better served by the love you have and the best intentions your child has in this very moment.

Surrender whatever is happening. Fighting it will only escalate your actions and amp up the intensity. See it, acknowledge it, and let it go. Don't give it any more power by being swayed by its intensity or over-thinking its characteristics. Remind yourself, "This is just something that is happening now." The ability to see very clearly the truth of the moment, without any filters or screens or overlays, will reveal your heart and the best way through it. Fear is an emotion best kept out of problem-solving because it does not contribute to a level-head. Learn how to focus and stay in the present and you will increase your chances of a peaceful resolution.

When my daughter fell apart despite my best attempts, I was so afraid that it was always going to be like that. I thought she would never relax and let me help her. It created so much anxiety that fueled my sense of hopelessness. Desperation wasn't far behind. Once I released that fear I could meet her where she was and be the calm presence she needed. Everything shifted. She didn't need someone desperate. She needed patience and someone who believed in her process. I learned to see every moment as an opportunity to connect rather than a chance to fail.

Universal Principle 2

Create Space

Sometimes we're like directors of a long-running improv show and it can feel exhausting. Anything can happen! If we provide some scripts they might help us get to the point sooner. They might take some weight off because we have a pretty good idea of what's going to happen and where people will stand and how the timing will impact our other productions. Except parenting isn't that straight-forward.

In our attempts to manage our kids, we lose the magic of spontaneity. When we set the path, we close the avenue to what else we might have seen. In the same way, when we issue directions and rules we miss out on what we might have discovered together. Or even what they may have stumbled upon on their own. That joy of discovery is incredibly meaningful and personal and it creates connection. It's through shared stories and inside jokes that we forge our bonds, our unique knowingness. By navigating difficult times together, we learn how to *be* together. We notice each other's subtle cues, hear the changes in voice, see the fleeting smiles and grimaces.

Rather than shutting down, open up. Considering trading the way you insist it to be for a negotiation. What possibilities exist outside of what you've already done? Do your kids have some good ideas to bring to the table, based on their feelings and needs? Getting it straight from the source can save you from misconstruing or misunderstanding. Before you jump to conclusions, take some time to investigate or wonder. Instead of automatically offering your solution, give your child a chance to come up with his own.

Create space where life can happen. Soften the edges of rigid rules and stretch them to make a place that embraces communication, mistakes, forgiveness, laughter, playfulness, experimentation and exploration. There is surprise in letting things unfold naturally and rolling with it; you can wind up in an unexpected place that has a new insight for you, a new perspective, a new understanding. Let it happen by being willing to allow it in. Be open to what you don't know and surrender to how it may change you or your child.

On your calendar, leave open time. Unscheduled buffers between appointments and activities so you can slow down and appropriately tend to your child. Make those openings so you can respond in the ways you want rather than hastily issuing commands. Also, with plenty of time, you allow for unexpected detours, spontaneous drop-ins and lingering visits. In other words, you invite life.

An open hand can offer. A tightly clenched one crushes. If you were your child which hand would you like to be held by? Open up that place where anything can happen and trust that you will come out the other side intact, maybe better. What possibilities can you create as you work through conflicting times?

When my daughter cried uncontrollably, I just wanted her to stop because it felt like I was doing something wrong. I also wanted to comfort her and help her feel better. When my attempts to hold her, rock her, nurse her or distract her didn't work, I was sure I was failing. Once I learned to stop trying to fix it, I opened a space for her to simply cry. I stayed as close as she would allow me but I didn't try to get her to stop, trusting that she had a reason I didn't understand. She learned how to feel her feelings completely and release them them she was done with them. I was there, offering my arms. When she was ready, she crawled into them for the most meaningful comfort of our relationship. It felt amazing to know that I could be her soft place to land, that she trusted me, that I made things better by not using force. The more we danced that dance, the fewer and farther between the episodes became. She became less intense as she learned to navigate her feelings from her own center rather than my direction.

Universal Principle 3

Break Through, Not Down

Stay strong. Don't give up. It doesn't have to spiral down into a mess on the floor. It may, but you don't have to help it there. You don't have to end up there. Get to the other side or climb higher than where you began, but resolve to not fall apart. It's not helpful to lose control of your emotions to the point that you can't contain them. Nothing feels more hopeless than being taken for a ride by frustration, anger and fear. Find a way to keep yourself in check until you can be alone to release it. That may mean taking a moment away from the situation before you blow. That's okay.

Remember your intention. Are you heading in a direction that will result in a happy, confident and capable family? Remember, you may need to surrender some of your ideas of how you will get there. Issuing punishments, discipline and lines in the sand will push your child to the breaking point. What will break? Your patience, your boundaries, your ability to calmly and rationally connect. Her composure, her trust, her sense of adventure and curiosity. If she learns to be afraid of you, she'll stop. Shutting down is not what you are after here so tread lightly. Know the difference between compliance and cooperation, well-behaved and content.

You and your child have the freedom to choose and the freedom to change your minds. Opt for mutually agreeable decisions with flexibility for what may arise. In choosing to work through moments together with your child, you are setting the course to work together. You *are* in this together, for better or worse, more committed than any marriage. This home you are tending can be full of confusion and anger or overflowing with fun and light-heartedness. You decide. There may be moments that are tough as your child is learning how to be in the world. It won't always be that way and it may be shorter-lived than you can even imagine. Either way, do your part to uplift and lighten the load. It's not necessary to get dragged to the bottom. It is possible to break *through*, not break *down*.

I specifically remember the day I understood the difference. I had cried through my morning shower and was still sobbing as I dried my hair. Tears streaming down my face, I caught a glimpse of myself in the mirror. I looked as bad as I felt and I thought to myself, *am I having a break down?* I caught my breath at the thought and immediately my answer raced to my heart. *No, you are having a break **through**.* I was just beginning to face some deeper truths that I had avoiding, confronting my fears, and admitting that falling apart was more convenient than bending. I didn't want to break, though, and I committed to getting to the other side of my fear. Through some introspection, I understood that things weren't as bad as I felt. Old hurts were impacting my ability to be in the present moment. That was the breakthrough that led me to remember the mother I really was - calm, strong and loving. By separating the past from the present, I could deal with each appropriately. I had been trying to avoid my pain but, in the end, the only way was through it. If I had broken down, my family would have broken as well.

What is holding you back? How can you break through it? Resolve to not be broken down, beaten down. Pick yourself up by your bootstraps, dust off the remnants and stare into your own eyes. How do you want it to be? Don't stop until you get there.

Universal Principle 4

Drop the Baggage (Not in Their Lap)

Our life experience can be very insightful. We learn a lot from where we've been. It can also be very heavy. Poor relationships, high expectations, failures, losses, abuse, trauma, grief - all of these contribute to how we relate to our present. Left unresolved, old negative experiences poison our best efforts to move on. We may not even realize how deeply we are still affected; we may not be able to see the harmful influence on our parenting.

We drag it in with us, from this relationship to the next. It shows up in our short tempers, our inability to let things slide, our desire to not make any mistakes. Our commitment to raising kids who won't ever feel the way we felt. To keep them on the right track, to keep their feet grounded and their heads on straight. When they are born, we vow to protect them.

We add another bag to our already heavy load. We pack it with all of the things we want to avoid. The things that we will never let happen. The rules and the authority that will keep everyone safe. The information overload as we research what's best. We've carried so much for so long, we think we can handle the extra baggage. However, we can't anticipate the pressure it creates. We can't see how it's crushing us, crushing our kids. Unwittingly, we've asked them to carry our bags with us. They are the ones who have to live up to our expectations by walking the path we've envisioned. They are the ones who are being measured and compared and evaluated and fussed over. Big weights for tiny shoulders. They aren't obligated to carry it nor are they prepared.

So just drop it.

All of those bags, all of that obligation and fear. It's not yours to carry anymore. You're here. How you got here doesn't matter to your children.

You can move more freely and more comfortably without the weight. Decide to put down everything that drags you down, holds you in place, prevents you from going to new places.

Don't hand it off to your child, either. It's not his or her responsibility to make sure your fears are not realized. It's not his or her job to achieve your ideal. It's not his or her job to reach all of those bars that have been set your whole life. It's not his or her job to pick up where you left off. That's *your* life. You deal with your stuff and let your child create and achieve his or her own standard. Give him or her a fresh start. Give yourself a fresh start.

How about you pack a new bag? This one is lightweight and nearly empty. It contains love, curiosity, and a sense of adventure. That's all you need to explore the bending curves and rolling hills with your children. Fill in the pockets with new stories, new discoveries, new memories. Don't forget to take a few photos along the way to show the grandkids. Happy trails lie ahead.

Universal Principle 5

Be the Mom You Want to Be

In every action you take, in every word you speak, you have the power to be whatever you choose. I encourage you to choose to be the mom you know you want to be. Not the mom you think you should be or the mom your friends are or the mom you've stumbled into. Decide with each word to be what you know to be nurturing, loving and helpful. Choose kindness. You didn't become a mom to be a martyr or a meanie. I'm guessing you wanted to mother a child because it feels good to love someone, to take care of them, to see them do things you never did. So do those things.

Remember what it feels like to look up to your mom. You did at one point in your life, probably still do in some ways. At the very least, you have a better understanding of her challenges and best intentions. Your child is going to look at you someday, too, with admiration. What will he say to his friends or partner about you? What do you want her to reflect back upon? Be that mom.

Will you be a partner or an authority? As you work through challenges together, you have an opportunity to show your child that you care about who he is, what he thinks, what he dreams of, what he can do. This is a chance to give him confidence in himself, develop critical thinking, look for alternatives, think for himself. Treating him as someone you value and respect shows him that he is worthy of those important building blocks. Listening to him express himself aids his understanding of his place in the world. Allowing him to be a part of the process demonstrates his significance as an individual.

When we make mistakes, we can slip easily into believing we can't do better. Even though we know we can, it can feel hopeless and we convince ourselves our ideal mothering skills are out of reach. Forgive yourself for the bad moments and try again. Giving up is the surest way to the status quo, and if you are looking to improve a situation, it requires your attention. You may need reminders, a support group, a daily practice to keep you on track. Do that. Set yourself up for success! Perhaps you'll need to cut back on something else. Maybe you just need to breathe before reacting. Would a mantra help?

I danced on the edge of anger often. It wasn't who I wanted to be - or who I really was - and it was caused by feelings that had nothing to do with my child. Yet, it still caused me to lash out in ways that were inconsistent with everything I knew, needed and desired. When I yelled I felt awful beyond words. It wasn't me, but I felt powerless to stop it because it seemed bigger than what I could control. So I stopped trying to do everything right every time. In each moment that I felt ready to pounce, I took a breath and asked myself *what kind of mom do you want to be?* The answer was always a kind, happy, helpful, understanding, loving, gentle one. When I saw that in my mind's eye it was easy for me to back down. That question repeatedly helped me through until I didn't need it anymore. I don't have to try to be that mom because I already am and it pours forth in all I do.

What kind of mom do you want to be? Instead of yelling, spanking or punishing, be that mom instead.

Step 1: Stop Before You Start

How to Calm Down

. . . .

What You Will Learn

° How to Interrupt a Poor Reaction   ° How to Find Calm in Chaos

° How to Regain your Confidence   ° How to Set your Intentions

° How to Use your Body and Senses

. . . .

You need a center from which to operate. Responses need to come from a clear, confident, calm mind. Scattered, impulsive, emotional reactions block your way. When a situation arises or you begin to feel triggered, this is the step you need first. You may need only a quick breath or you may need to employ several techniques. It doesn't matter; just make sure you take a moment to check in with yourself before you open your mouth or move to act. None of us want to lash out but it can happen.

It's easy to be caught off guard.

We can snap without knowing we were on edge.

We can be interrupted at a critical moment.

We can be confused, tired, not feeling 100%.

We may be surprised by the suddenness of a reaction with a bewildered, *where did that come from and why is this happening?*

Don't try to think in that space because it won't be an honest reflection of your priorities. The good news is that we can do better - it's not too late. At your core, you are a loving, nurturing, protective mother. That's the place from which you want to respond when communicating with your child.

When we're upset, depending on our personalities, it can take some time to calm down.

Take it! Don't rush through this process. It's worth it to assess yourself before you assess the situation. You can easily tangle your emotions with your child's emotions and with whatever may be happening making a big jumbled heap of helplessness.

It might not take more than a second to breathe and shake the residue of where your head was a moment before. Clear yourself in whatever manner works best for you.

This Helps Accomplish

° Connecting vs. Conflicting

° Opening Up vs. Shutting Up

° a Happy Ending vs. a Teary Showdown

° Moving Closer vs. Pushing Away

It can be helpful to think about this before the moment strikes so you can quickly access what you need. If you have thoughts or guiding principles, find a way to keep them in the front of your mind or have a way to quickly pull them from the back of your mind. Some of the prompts in this step will help you do that.

From the beginning, you can prepare yourself for what may come and orient yourself in a calm and clear direction.

When a conflict arises, it feels good to know you'll be able to achieve happy endings and not regrets. When you know what works for you it makes it easy to slip into that place of peaceful presence. Direction helps balance us when we're uncertain or out of control and provides a toolkit so we don't have to scramble to think in the heat of the moment.

The turning point came for me when I learned how to stop before I started. My daughter would do something that triggered me and I could feel my harsh reaction rising quickly to the surface. There was no barrier between my impulse to yell and her sweet face that would receive it. I could see her standing there in all her tender innocence that meant everything to me and still let it all loose. Once I started, I couldn't stop myself even when I wanted to. Afterward, I felt like the worst mother in the world and would grieve for all that had been lost in that moment - our opportunity to connect, her trust in me and sense that I was a safe person to come to, the message of love that I wanted to send instead. It was awful to feel this way. I beat myself up over and over for reacting in a way that did not match my values and the overwhelming love I had for my daughter. All of that self-loathing did not change anything for me.

That's when I began to understand that if I wanted to affect the way it ended, I had to affect the way it began. I needed to get back in touch with how I really felt about my daughter instead of how I was feeling triggered. I needed to get back to gratitude for the opportunity to help her navigate life, learning how to be in relationship with others. I needed to remind myself of my role as a nurturing, helpful person.

If you can feel good at the beginning, you have a better chance of feeling good at the end.

The goal is to respond calmly not react harshly. *What would that look like for you? What might it look like for your child?* Many a situation can be soothed by just helping them stop before they start. As you are slowing down, invite your child to slow down with you by opening the door to what works for them. For example, my daughter calmed down by nursing. I calmed down by holding her. Win/Win.

Let's explore some action ideas you can use immediately.

1

Be Quiet

Give yourself a moment to collect your thoughts. It's easy to just blurt out an immediate reaction that may send things heading in the wrong direction. Just zip it for a few seconds while you orient yourself. Try to extend the quiet from your toes to your head, from your breath to your thoughts. Don't say anything.

Mantra: Find Stillness

Try this: Don't say anything

Avoid: Over-reacting

2

Breathe

If you're breathing you can't say something you don't want to say. You are also creating a parasympathetic response in your body that calms you. With a few good breaths, you can decrease your blood pressure, heart rate and muscle tension. Your mind calms and your body feels at ease. Be sure they are deep, steady breaths. Short and shallow breathing can stir up your thoughts and create anxiety. For best results, take three long, slow breaths through your nose. Fill your lower lungs first, then your upper lungs until you feel your belly and ribs expand.

Mantra: Deep Breaths

Try this: Count to five while you inhale

Avoid: Clenching your jaw

3

Change the Scenery

External stimuli can heighten emotions for everyone. If it's busy, loud, crowded or chaotic, move to another location that is calmer. Don't let yourself or your child remain overstimulated. It's harder to remain calm when your environment is working against you. Also, if there is something in your surroundings that is causing the problem, it can help to remove it. For example, my daughter once wanted a stuffed animal that I had very good reasons not to buy. As long as we were in that store and she could see the object of her desire, she couldn't calm herself enough to listen to me. I carried her out of the store and to the car where there were no fluffy distractions and we both had an opportunity to calm down and talk. Change the focus.

Mantra: Go to a Calmer Place

Try this: Mute the background noise

Avoid: Feeling trapped

4

Close your Eyes

Block out the scene. When your child looks distressed, it triggers your panic buttons. As a mother our first instinct is to protect our kids and often that looks like Just Making It Stop. We think that if we can eliminate the pain, everything will be okay. But that quick reaction is a shortcut and you will be overlooking so many other parts of the puzzle. You can curb that impulse by simply closing your eyes for a second to gain your balance and prepare yourself for working through it. Staring at what troubles you will not help.

Mantra: It's not as bad as it looks.

Try this: Look up; it helps open your chest so you can breathe easier, too.

Avoid: Being overstimulated

Touch Their Head

Mothers have an intimate, physical connection with our kids. We spent so much time touching their sweet little heads when they were babies. Those were magical moments that held so much hope and promise. We can easily be reminded of the love we have for them by re-connecting to those days by touching them. Also by putting your hand on that head, you realize just how small they are; how much they are growing. They need you, Mom, so be there for them and help them navigate this tricky stage of development.

Mantra: This is my baby here.

Try this: Rest your cheek on his/her head and breathe.

Avoid: Forgetting who they are.

6

Count

This isn't meant to be used to get your child to do something within three or five or ten seconds. Use this old trick to buy time for yourself. While you're counting you are giving your body a chance to relax as you breathe. You're giving the moment an opportunity to shift. If counting to ten isn't enough, keep going until you feel ready. Do it in your head so your child doesn't think you are threatening him. You'll be surprised how many situations and feelings resolve themselves in under a minute.

Mantra: One, two, three, breathe, four...

Try this: Count backwards

Avoid: Reacting too soon

7

Stop

Don't be impulsive. Instead, take a break, give it a second, think it over. Just hold it until you can move on to another strategy. By not reacting immediately, you are opening the door to other possibilities. Your first reaction doesn't have to be acted upon. You have other choices so give them a chance to surface.

Mantra: Wait a second.

Try this: Hold up your hand

Avoid: Barreling ahead

8

Don't Take it Personally

Do you feel that this is your fault or that you are being blamed? Let it go. You may have contributed to the situation but taking on feelings of shame will serve to knock you off your center. You can't operate successfully from that place. Even when it looks like you've played a part, likely there is an underlying reason for your child's extreme reaction. Release your feelings of guilt and don't be defensive. Jumping to conclusions and placing accusations leads to more problems. Be open to what's really happening instead of blaming yourself. It's possible that your child's reaction or behavior is a result of something internal. Don't own that. Let it be hers so you can help her through it. This is not a reflection of your character or ability.

Mantra: This isn't about me.

Try this: Imagine a shield of protection

Avoid: Getting defensive

9

Smile

Another simple way to lift your mood. When you smile, you feel better instantly. When you smile you also reassure those around you that you aren't going to blow. This simple act inspires you to act happy and be happy rather than angry. A mean face isn't very welcoming and doesn't invite conversation. Open the space by showing you are willing to be there. It's your choice to be a mad mother or a friendly, helpful one. A smile will remind you of who you are and the happiness you want to have.

Mantra: Smiling feels better.

Try this: Notice how your face feels

Avoid: Furrowing your brow

10

Remember Your Achievements

You can get through this. You've dealt with a problem before and lived to tell the tale, right? I'm willing to bet that you've had a few successful outcomes, too. This won't knock you down, and if you take your time you'll get better and better at negotiating tricky situations. What have you achieved? Bolster yourself with memories of dancing yourself to 1st place in the talent show; negotiating that real estate contract; getting a job; moving away from home; trying that surfing lesson; picking yourself up after a break-up; deciphering your baby's cries. Translate your abilities to your current objective of building thriving relationships. If you can approach this as a practice, you'll develop patience and invest in the process. You've got the skills to be a great mom.

Mantra: I can do anything.

Try this: Imagine your courage to try

Avoid: Believing this is too hard

11

Be Grateful You're Together

Your child is a gift and you can be a gift to your child. Before you go diving into a discussion, take a minute to recognize how blessed you are to have this opportunity. There is a living, breathing child in front of you needing your help. Remember that one day your child will be grown and gone. The days that are yours to directly impact his confidence and self-esteem tick down with each setting sun. Don't waste the time you have together. Don't throw it away in a fit of indignation, anger, confusion, authority or power. This is a chance to powerfully connect in love. Gratitude can pull you out of whatever upset, disappointment or fear is building in you.

Mantra: I'm glad he/she's here.

Try this: See him/her as a gift to you

Avoid: Throwing your gift away

My Own Action Idea

Mantra:

Try this:

Avoid:

My Own Action Idea

Mantra:

Try this:

Avoid:

CONSIDERATIONS

Stop Before You Start

What do you want to avoid doing or saying?

_____
_____
_____
_____
_____
_____
_____
_____

What are you willing to do to work through this?

_____
_____
_____
_____
_____
_____
_____
_____

List some ways that you calm down. What do you need? (a breath, quiet, food, time?)

_____
_____
_____
_____
_____
_____
_____
_____

CONSIDERATIONS

What are some obstacles to you using these? How can you work around them?

_____
_____
_____
_____
_____
_____
_____
_____
_____

What are the biggest issues you face relating to your child?

_____
_____
_____
_____
_____
_____
_____
_____
_____

Are these issues truly as big as they feel or is your perspective skewed by other factors? (eg: it may be so intense that it seems like it happens more than it does.)

_____
_____
_____
_____
_____
_____
_____
_____

44

CONSIDERATIONS

Is your child sensitive to external stimuli?

_____
_____
_____
_____
_____
_____
_____
_____

What calms your child? How do they like to relax? What do they respond happily to?

_____
_____
_____
_____
_____
_____
_____
_____

How can you implement these tools prior to stressful situations or as your child becomes upset?

_____
_____
_____
_____
_____
_____
_____
_____

CONSIDERATIONS

What triggers you? Are you sensitive to external stimuli, such as noise, clutter, too many people, small spaces, etc? What can you do to avoid this or help yourself quickly when it occurs?

_____
_____
_____
_____
_____
_____
_____
_____

Which of your reactions do you want to change?

_____
_____
_____
_____
_____
_____
_____
_____

Are you quick to anger or does it build? What's the process like?

_____
_____
_____
_____
_____
_____
_____
_____

CONSIDERATIONS

Do you have large challenges in your life that are affecting your ability to be calm, have time and space to think and spend quality time with your child? What are they and how can you get help?

_____
_____
_____
_____
_____
_____
_____
_____
_____

What are your values? What's important to you as a mother?

_____
_____
_____
_____
_____
_____
_____
_____
_____

In your ideal world, how would you respond to your child's requests and challenges?

_____
_____
_____
_____
_____
_____
_____
_____

CONSIDERATIONS

What would it be like for your child to experience that? How would they see you?

_____
_____
_____
_____
_____
_____
_____
_____

How will this ideal response benefit your relationship?

_____
_____
_____
_____
_____
_____
_____
_____

Our ideal world may be out of reach, but don't let that stop you from trying to get there. Tell yourself that you can always do better.

_____
_____
_____
_____
_____
_____
_____
_____

Step 2: Identify the Problem Without Yelling and Jumping to Conclusions

How to Objectively Understand

. . . .

What You Will Learn

° How to Understand what you want to Resolve

° How to Know if you are on the Right Track

° Ways to Find a Solution

° How to Set Goals

. . . .

Do you find yourself in the midst of something you don't understand?

Why is she so upset?

What does this mean?

How can I get it to stop?

What will happen if this continues?

We don't always know and we may never figure it out. Does that mean that we can't or shouldn't always try to learn what we can? Let's do our best to uncover any meaning that is available to us to assist our problem-solving.

We come to parenting with biases. Judging others for indulgence, not enough attention, too much junk food, not enough structure, etc...we have all the answers. We're sure of all the right ways while we steer clear of the wrong ones, dragging the way we were raised into our ideas. Or maybe we've read all the books and have put our faith so rigidly in what the experts say that we know exactly what to do. Then we have kids who don't seem to respond well to those models and we think we just aren't doing it enough. We say to ourselves, *Be more consistent- you're on the right path, you just aren't doing it enough.* Because we believe we already know what's right, we don't devote much effort to examining the cause of the problem. We use our pre-conceived notions without considering other possible reasons or ideas. This makes us inflexible and can contribute to a lack of progress or even a downward spiral.

Another scenario is that we are sure we know our kids. In fact, we're often told that we know them better than anyone else. "You know them best." They change, though. And your second child is not your first child; oftentimes, they're polar opposites. We see what we want to see and we can, in fact, cloud reality with our own version of it without even knowing it. We make assumptions without understanding that something has changed or that we were just plain wrong to begin with.

> ## This Helps Accomplish
>
> ° Objectivity and Clarity
>
> ° New Perspectives
>
> ° Less Spiraling Down
>
> ° a Foundation for Honest and Effective Communication

It's important to separate fact from fiction from good intentions.

If we aren't occasionally seeing with new eyes and objective openness, we may not know our kids at all.

If we take it a step further and label our kids, we are short-cutting our understanding. If we jump to the conclusion, for example, that "she just cries to get attention," or "he always bullies her," or "she's just so shy," we are missing an opportunity to learn what else may be true.

When might you need help identifying a problem? There may be an argument between siblings or friends. Dangerous behavior such as hitting, biting or causing other physical harm. Emotional issues like bullying or anger. Relationships that feel difficult- poor communication, lying, feeling the need to force, control or punish. Meltdowns and unexpected reactions. Struggling when leaving the house. Extreme resistance to requests. Kids who just don't seem happy. You might not feel happy. In our effort to take care of things quickly, it's easy to yell or jump to conclusions.

> ## Avoid this
>
> It is tempting to let your child "figure it out on her own." Sometimes a child can and as they get older, her ability and desire to do so grows. However, as the parent, it is your job to help them navigate the world of relationships and challenges. Remember, their bodies and minds may not have the ability yet. They can look more mature than they are. In other instances, they just haven't had enough experience. Don't let them flail around trying to figure things out. Wouldn't you appreciate a helping hand?

I remember a day when my kids were building castles with their blocks. They were happy until I heard a loud crash and my little one crying. Rushing to the room, I saw her writhing on the floor so upset and angry, trying to get at her sister. Knowing that she liked to knock her buildings down herself, I assumed that her sister had done it, thus causing the conflict. All I wanted in that moment was to make the anger and crying stop. I thought that if the little one could see that I was taking care of the situation, she would feel better. I offered to re-build the castle so she could knock it down herself. That just fanned the flames and I was so confused and exasperated.

Eventually, I figured out that I had jumped to the wrong conclusion because of past experience and because I thought I knew my daughter so well. In reality, she was upset because she knocked her blocks down, expecting them to fall in a certain way. It had nothing to do with her sister or anything else. I learned something new that day: when her expectations fail to be met, she feels out of control. When she feels out of control, she loses control. This new information helped me prepare her to expect more than one possible outcome, reducing her vulnerability in many situations. The incidence of sadness and anger caused by disappointment was significantly reduced.

Don't confuse irritations, differing preferences, and inexperience with problems to be fixed. See it as helpful information.

Keep this in mind: Having more information does not mean that things will always change quickly. Spilled milk on a new dress is easier to understand and work through than feeling like a middle child who doesn't get enough attention.

Also remember: you won't know everything; you can't solve everything. You may just need to let it go or again, lend a helping hand until age and experience kicks in.

By understanding the problem at hand you can create a road map to solutions. By opening communication you gain clarity. By going deep you can reveal if this is a major or minor issue and identify to what it may be related. By creating perspective you can prioritize what needs your attention the most. By focusing on what's really happening vs. what you may be perceiving you can more accurately identify what you want to solve.

Let's explore some action ideas you can use immediately.

12

Ask

Don't jump to conclusions. Find out exactly what happened by asking and actively listening. It's easy to fall back on the past and carry that into the moment. It's good to rely on what you know while at the same time being open to what may be different this time. Each moment is unique and it's important to treat it as such. It only takes a moment to clarify and it's better to have more information to work with. You build trust when your child recognizes that you are not making assumptions. Ask probing questions of everyone involved until you have a clear understanding. Explain any differences you are hearing between all points of view. Give an opportunity to correct statements and you'll get a pretty good snapshot of what's happening.

Mantra: Let's find out.

Try this: Repeat it back for clarity

Avoid: Having a pre-conceived bias

Forget What You Know

It's not always what you think it is. Toss out the conflicting books you've read or ideas with which you were raised. You may know your child well enough to have some pretty strong clues about what's going on, but give them the benefit of the doubt by being willing to hear another side. You may uncover something that has been overlooked or that your child was unable to articulate before. Something may have changed. This is an opportunity to expand your knowledge. It's also a time to recognize how your child and your relationship is evolving. Provide a space for new ideas to surface.

Mantra: Maybe it's something else.

Try this: Have an open ear

Avoid: Being stubborn

14

Talk it Out

Take some time to verbalize what's happening. It develops communication skills and the ability to be clear and calm. It also provides a platform for your child to express themselves and their ideas. It's empowering to contribute and it will encourage them to solve problems independently. The more experience a child has in presenting facts, thoughts and feelings, the stronger those muscles become. A pattern can develop over time that replaces less desirable behaviors. Most importantly, talking *with* your child instead of *to* him, reinforces the idea that you are on his side, willing to work together. This builds safety, security and confidence.

Mantra: Let's talk about it.

Try this: "So, what you're saying is..."

Avoid: Doing all the talking

15

Reconsider

Generally a child who is acting out, is acting out. That is to say that they need something. Reconsider the notion that meltdowns, arguing and physical aggression are the problem. There is something else trying to be heard, trying to be healed, trying to be helped. You might think that it's just about the broken toy but it could be about feeling a lack of control over the environment or the disappointment with the discovery that someone else has power over your precious objects. Gain a perspective that your child is trying to tell you something important behind the scenes.

Mantra: This is just a symptom.

Try this: Look beneath the surface

Avoid: Focusing on the wrong thing

See It's Not About You

This present moment isn't about how you've failed as a parent. It's not about how you made the wrong choice. It's about a person who's learning and needs your assistance. The focus needs to be on what the situation at hand is needing, not blame and self-critique. Don't contribute to the situation by piling on emotions that don't belong there. You already feel overwhelmed, right? Don't make it worse. When you take your own bad feelings out of the equation you clear the way to understanding the underlying factors that you can affect. Sometimes those factors include your feelings but, at this stage of the game, stay objective and not emotional.

Mantra: This isn't about me.

Try this: Imagine a pause button for your emotions

Avoid: Assigning blame

17

What's Missing?

What expectation hasn't been met? If you're eating dinner is his favorite cup missing? In what ways have you not been paying attention or providing what's needed or wanted? Have you spent enough time together? Is his sweater too hot? A seam too itchy? Need a bathroom break? Have the big muscle groups been exercised enough? Did you pack everything you needed? When was the last snack? Was sleep lacking last night? Is it physical? Emotional? What are you not seeing that could be a contributing factor?

Mantra: What has been overlooked?

Try this: Scan the physical environment first then re-trace your steps

Avoid: Missing easy fixes

Try

Make an honest effort to understand what's happening. Listen closely, ask good questions. Be patient. Help your child relax and open up to you. Stop what you're doing and put her on your lap, look her in the eyes. Tune in and focus on what's happening. This isn't a time to be half-hearted. Using your full attention is like using all of your senses while eating a good meal: you'll enjoy it more, take more in, create a positive emotional response and feel satisfied at the end.

Mantra: I want to do this.

Try this: Take one step

Avoid: Not giving it enough time

Identify Feelings

Feeling angry is different from feeling disappointed yet they can look the same. You can't know how to deal with a situation until you know exactly what feeling you're facing. A surface emotion can be hiding layers of feelings and until you get to the root cause, you won't be effective. You can nip something in the bud but it will grow back. Get to the real issue by reflecting back what you're seeing. "So you're feeling x because of y? What does it make you want to do?" An angry child could benefit from learning ways to dissipate the anger. A sad child might need some cuddles and time to be heard. Learning to differentiate emotions can help kids know themselves and what they need. It's a process, though.

Mantra: What's the real feeling?

Try this: "Does your body feel tight or floppy?"

Avoid: Confusing similar symptoms

Decide What's Important

What happened, happened. It's time to move on and improve the relationship. Is anything more important than your child? His feelings? His perspective on the world? No, there isn't. Your child needs you to believe he is your priority. This creates deep security and self-esteem, critical building blocks for any person. What are you willing to let go of to preserve what matters most? Reputation, authority, attachment to belongings, history? Let's focus on what's really happening and the effects it is having on the involved parties. Decide to make things better right now, not in some elusive future.

Mantra: S/he's more important to me than this.

Try this: Will this matter in ten years?

Avoid: Getting your priorities mixed up

Choose the Relationship

In every interaction you have the opportunity to build connection, trust and safety. The relationship is paramount! It is more important than placing blame, saving face or issuing punishment. Those tactics tear down what you are trying to build. Don't you always want your child to feel free to come to you, especially when they are teenagers and their curiosities have bigger outcomes? It starts when she is young and the chances of her coming to you increase every time you sit with her and explore what she is thinking and feeling. Take her seriously and she'll take you seriously. Be willing to hear her side and she'll be willing to hear yours.

Mantra: The relationship is #1.

Try this: Do one sweet thing

Avoid: Pushing him or her away

22

Know Your Limit

At what point will you lose it? What is your biggest trigger? It's always important to keep everyone safe and knowing what it going to send you over the edge is the best way to do that. Be ready to walk away or breathe, etc. when you are getting close to unravelling. What can you handle and when do *you* need help?

Mantra: I can handle this for a while.

Try this: When I get to ___, I walk away.

Avoid: Doing something you'll regret

23

Is it Reversible?

Identify where the train ran off the tracks. If it's something that can be fixed by starting over, start over. If you said something you want to take back, take it back. Don't be afraid to stop where you are - mid-sentence even. In the same way, think ahead and don't make a choice you will wish you could reverse. You can't un-spank a child. The red mark may fade, but the effect will linger. If it's reversible, go back. If it's not reversible, and you've already made a mistake, apologize, make it clear that your child doesn't deserve that treatment and commit to never doing it again.

Mantra: Can I get a do-over?

Try this: Rewind and Try Again

Avoid: Getting farther away from your goal

Bend, Don't Break

Be willing to extend yourself. It's easy to be overwhelmed. Solutions aren't always apparent and sometimes you don't have a lot of information to use. Be supple. Be willing to accept that you won't always figure out the problem or the cause. Maybe all you can do this time is deal with the effect it's having and come back to it later when the smoke has cleared. Don't give up and resort to an arbitrary punishment or withdrawing in a way that will only create isolation. The last thing a child needs is to feel abandoned when they need you. Rally your resources and offer your lap, your silence, your tender, loving care. Soften into that.

Mantra: I am flexible.

Try this: Shake out your limbs

Avoid: Snapping and withdrawing love

My Own Action Idea

Mantra:

Try this:

Avoid:

My Own Action Idea

Mantra:

Try this:

Avoid:

CONSIDERATIONS

For ongoing behaviors/concerns: How often does this happen?

_____
_____
_____
_____
_____
_____
_____

When does it happen?

_____
_____
_____
_____
_____
_____
_____

What does it look like (crying, hitting, bullying, demanding)?

_____
_____
_____
_____
_____
_____
_____
_____

CONSIDERATIONS

How does it feel to you? During? After? What does it tell you you need? What's your limit?

_____

_____

_____

_____

_____

_____

_____

_____

_____

How does it feel to your child? During? After? What does it tell you s/he needs?

_____

_____

_____

_____

_____

_____

_____

_____

_____

What may you be overlooking or forgetting to do?

_____

_____

_____

_____

_____

_____

_____

CONSIDERATIONS

What else might be going on? Look beyond the surface behavior or obvious cause.

_____
_____
_____
_____
_____
_____
_____
_____

How will you create an environment and a relationship where your child feels comfortable talking to you?

_____
_____
_____
_____
_____
_____
_____
_____

How might your own reactions and behavior be causing, contributing to or escalating behaviors or situations?

_____
_____
_____
_____
_____
_____
_____

CONSIDERATIONS

Present Reality-----------|-----------|-----------|----------Desired Reality

Small   Medium   Large

What would a small improvement look like?

_____
_____
_____
_____
_____
_____
_____
_____
_____

What would a medium improvement look like?

_____
_____
_____
_____
_____
_____
_____
_____
_____

What would a large improvement look like?

_____
_____
_____
_____
_____
_____
_____

Identify the Problem

Step 3: Identify Accountability

How to Stop Blaming and Get the Truth

. . . .

What You Will Learn

° How to Reduce Arguments   ° How to Improve Relationships

° How to Eliminate Blame   ° How to Reduce Punishment

. . . .

When we get fired up, it's important to understand what or who is really responsible. Often we complicate situations by dragging in irrelevant things and we end up inappropriately blaming our child.

Old thoughts and feelings and experiences can be triggered quite easily without even knowing it. When we confuse what is happening right now with a past experience, we muddy the water and create obstacles where there aren't any. It's very easy to behave as if we are still in that old experience instead of a current time with new circumstances.

We generally represent our history unless we make a conscious, aware effort to be in the present moment.

Today is not the same as yesterday.

It's from your adult perspective that you can separate the past from now; perception from reality; and current feelings from ancient hurts that contaminate your thoughts and actions. Keep each where they belong.

Have you ever considered how *your* experience as a child is different from *your child's* experience as a child? Think about that for a bit.

Notice the elements and experiences that do not resemble your childhood. This is how your child is growing in his unique way with his unique set of variables. This is a person who is encountering life differently than you did. How can you know his experience better? Can you see how his perspective differs from yours? What bothered you as a child may not be the same for him and vice versa.

What about how his or her present sense of being in the world is different from yours? Kids aren't concerned about clean floors and being on time, and they shouldn't be. They'll get there, don't worry. Obviously, you are not in the same life stage. Don't expect her to act like an adult just as you are not expected to act like a child. You and your body have had a lot more time to learn how to sit still, not interrupt, say thank you. Or maybe not? Maybe you or other adults you know still struggle with these things. We're all learning at our own pace.

> ## This Helps Accomplish
>
> ° Developing Honesty and Trust
>
> ° Creating Compassion and New Insights
>
> ° Deepening Connections
>
> ° An End to Repeat Issues

You have many diverse responsibilities on your plate. Your kid has one: to grow. You might have a million thoughts swirling through your mind right now. Your child probably just has one right now, but even if he has a couple, they're all probably different from yours. He's just a kid without all of your experience, filters and voices.

They are not you and you are not them.

It seems obvious but we get caught up in our own experience and forget. Remember to keep your internal dialogue or feelings out of it - this is about what's happening *for your child*. As you parent it is critically helpful to know what's honestly happening inside of a request, a behavior, a moment. Kids deserve the benefit of the doubt. They don't know what you know. Once you can establish roles and responsibilities, moving forward is much clearer and quicker. You don't have to butt heads over every little thing. Some conflicts are a result of assumptions and blame. You make assumptions based on how *you* would feel - that's not always accurate. Your old, awful feelings are stirred up and, instead of recognizing that, you blame whatever just happened to trigger you. Eliminate these barriers and you open the way to simple, peaceful resolutions.

Your child is not responsible for your feelings. Your anger is yours. Your disappointment is yours. Your frustration is yours. Wanting him to be x,y and z is yours. He just threw the toy. He just can't reason yet. He just wants more ice cream. He is who he is for right now. Whatever that triggers in you, however that makes you feel- it's not his fault. Handing that accountability over to a little boy will only cripple your ability to deal with the situation. Blaming him confuses the issue and harms your relationship. He suffers for your inability to cope and you suffer from feelings of guilt and inadequacy.

The hardest lesson I learned was that much of the angst I felt originated in me. I just wanted my daughter's expressed frustration to stop because I was afraid of what it meant. I was sure it was because I wasn't good enough or there was something terribly wrong with her and that just fed the cycle. Instead of just owning my frustration and fear and exploring where it was coming from, I got mad at her for crying and "making" me feel that way. *Doesn't she see that I am doing everything I can for her? Why is she doing this to me?* What a mess! The truth is that I escalated the problem because I was trying to escape my fear that something was going to go terribly wrong in our lives. I took responsibility for everything and I couldn't see that I wasn't giving us all enough time. My young daughter needed more of my attention, more time to transition, more of everything. My nerves were frayed and everything felt rushed because I didn't leave enough space for our needs. My daughter needed more time to finish playing, to eat, to get used to the idea that she was going to be sitting in the car seat. I needed more breathing room so I could be a loving and gentle mom; more headspace to see that I mostly was that mom but that I was just challenged in some moments; more understanding that everything happens when the time is right. I was actually contributing to the meltdowns and sometimes made them worse because I wouldn't respond calmly. I let my fear get stirred into the mix, unable to see that I had only confused and complicated the situation. Once I learned to own my part, life dramatically improved for us all.

Your job is to be the mature parent. Know which of your feelings are caused by the present situation and which are caused by life experiences with other family members, friends, lovers, teachers.

Your child's job is to be an ever-changing kid. He or she needs to learn how to solve problems and handle emotion. It takes time. He or she will have their own feelings and experiences. You child is not here to make you happy.

The beautiful part is that you get to access your experiences rationally to help your child move through theirs.

Let's explore some action ideas you can use immediately.

25

Open Your Heart

Share your experiences with your child so she doesn't feel alone in her experience. Be careful not to make it *about* you but do offer your comfort that it's happened before to other people. A very effective way to connect when she is spinning out of control is to identify with her. It gets her attention when someone admits to feeling angry or disappointed or confused. Rather than trying to distract from feelings, share yours. Try to use an example that doesn't include her so she doesn't think that you are associating your feeling with her. It is helpful, though, to talk about situations she is familiar with or to go directly inside her current moment. Tell her about how you felt when that happened to you. When you do this you can recognize blame has no place here.

Mantra: I can relate to this.

Try this: "This one time when I was..."

Avoid: Stuffing feelings away

26

Separate Your Thoughts

Your thoughts can be based on old stories and irrelevant to your present moment. So easily we derail ourselves by getting confused with negative thought patterns that result in words and actions that are not helpful. Remember that an awareness to quieting those old voices will go a long way towards hearing the truth - your child's truth. Listen carefully and stay focused on new thoughts about what you just heard; ignore old ideas that want to make this about something that it is not. You might think it's best for your child to clean their plate because you had to and you grew right on track. Let go of that power struggle by understanding that there are different appetites for different bodies. Evolve.

Mantra: What do I really think now?

Try this: "Where is this thought from?"

Avoid: Ideas that don't apply anymore

Separate Your Feelings

Take some time to check in with how you really feel. Our uncomfortable, old feelings can be easily lit by something that our child requests or does. Recognize old feelings when they arise and put them aside. Our children grow up in a different (perhaps similar) environment with different experiences, expectations, desires and needs. Consider how they might be feeling differently that you are. Where you may be nervous, they may be excited. You may be scared, they may be fearless. You may feel lacking, they may feel abundant. Also, consider that you aren't responding to what they are doing specifically but about how you are overwhelmed by too much of it, like noise. If you are highly sensitive, pay close attention to this.

Mantra: What am I really feeling now?

Try this: "Why am I feeling this?"

Avoid: Being unnecessarily emotional

28

Own Your Part

Be honest with how you have contributed to the situation. Was there something you overlooked or didn't communicate? Were you in a hurry and didn't plan well? Are you doing too much? Did you change your mind? Could you have done something differently? Have you provided enough food, exercise, play, opportunities to sleep? There's no shame in admitting you could have done it differently. This is a great opportunity to model taking responsibility with dignity and grace and without fear or guilt. Admit it, and take steps to rectify it while remembering to do better next time.

Mantra: That's on me this time.

Try this: Be honest, not ashamed

Avoid: Shifting blame

Remember Change & that Time Passes

Kids are learning all the time - it's their job. Your role is to let them do it naturally. Sometimes it's a white knuckle ride through the bumpy parts, but phases come and go. Bodies get bigger and more coordinated. Hormones shift and brains shape and re-shape causing and preventing many actions and abilities. Sometimes your child just isn't able to do or be what you want. With time, things change. It can be overnight or gradual. Some things are never going to go away, but they soften, you all learn how to see the gift, you figure things out. Don't discount the power of giving something time and allowing for change. Let your kids have the opportunity of learning as they go.

Mantra: This isn't forever.

Try this: Envision a learning curve

Avoid: Not seeing the bigger picture

30

Don't Play the Victim

It's not about you. That's your ego wanting attention, to feel needed and necessary. Learning to express oneself is an art and along the way things may be said or done that are not a good representation of what's really happening. You may be an easy target because you are there, you are safe and you aren't going anywhere. Our kids know they can experiment on us because they won't lose us no matter how it goes down. They aren't bullying, manipulating or trying to hurt you. They aren't *doing this to you*, they are learning who they are. Try to deflect those painful twinges that pop up and see your child's behavior for what it is: an attempt to get a need met. Your child is telling you what is needed but they might not always do it well. Don't take on the role of martyr.

Mantra: This is not meant to hurt me.

Try this: Envision it rolling off your skin

Avoid: Being dramatic

Grow

Parenting is the most important job you will ever have. This is a role you will have for the rest of your life. Doesn't it deserve as least as much time and energy that you give to other people and projects? Making the decision to become a parent puts the ball in your court to advance what you know, improve your skills and get better in your role. Just as our little ones start at the beginning, so do we. As they grow, so must we. In fact, the responsibility to lead the way is ours. See your interactions as an opportunity to do better. Take the time to learn what you can when it's calm, not when you're under pressure. Increase the time between conflicts by engaging happily with your child more often.

Mantra: I can do better.

Try this: Schedule time to work on one parenting skill every week

Avoid: Settling for average

32

Understand You Are Not In Control

Putting your best foot forward is not the same thing as controlling the outcome. Please do not see yourself as a puppeteer getting your child to do your dance. Control is an illusion that stands in the way of honest connection, lasting understanding and necessary evolution. It is not your job to make things go a certain way. No one really has that ability. We can be influencers and guides and path-lighters, but there are too many factors that are shaping your child's path to think that you can own it. Ultimately, it is their life and you are their life support. Find ways that you can move things in a peaceful, positive direction and then surrender to the possibilities that pop up along the way. Work to be prepared but know that you can't prepare for everything. A flexible, multi-faceted approach to parenting will serve you well.

Mantra: I can't force it.

Try this: Be inspiring

Avoid: Being "in charge"

33

Change History

It doesn't have to be the way it always was. You don't have to parent the way your parents did or the same way as all those experts you've followed. You don't have to continue to parent the way have been parenting. Remember again that your kids are not you and are not doomed to repeat history. You have the chance to do it differently, turn away from negativity or what you've learned doesn't work or what doesn't feel right. If it hurts, it's probably not helping. Change course knowing that you may experience some doubt and resistance, especially from family. Decide that the past doesn't have to be dragged into the present or contaminate the future. Give your kids the childhood you never had. It's not too late to begin again.

Mantra: I can change history.

Try this: Just say no to the status quo

Avoid: Giving your power to the past

34

Don't Pass It On

Identify what doesn't serve you and commit to letting it go. Lineage can be a blessing or a curse and the beautiful part is you get to decide which it will be for your kids. Make a list to identify all of the behaviors you don't want your kids to learn from you. These are probably the result of relationships stretching back generations or encounters with other adults in your young life. Coping techniques are not parenting methods. How good would it feel to know that you are not passing that hurt on? It goes no further than you as you discover new ways to experience life. When conflict arises, you don't have to give your kids the same lessons you learned the hard way. Grab their hand and find new lessons happily together, letting the past slip away.

Mantra: Don't pass this on.

Try this: Take responsibility for yourself

Avoid: Repeating the cycle

Inspire the Future

How will your kids describe their childhood? How will they describe you? Inspire laughter and confidence from adult children as they talk about the way they were raised. When they are parenting their own kids, will they want to channel your patience, your understanding and your compassion? Or will they be struggling to not pass on what hurt them? Keeping the big picture in mind is a great way to remove yourself from the intensity of a moment. Consider how this will all look in thirty years. What will matter? What will linger? What won't they ever forget?

Mantra: Do I want to be remembered for this?

Try this: Make happy memories

Avoid: Wishing it had been better

36

Know Who You Are

Beneath all of what you've learned and experienced in all of your years is your root self. What personality were you born with? Where or to what are you drawn? Before you were shaped and molded by life, you were pure love, curiosity, trust; innocent, free, unafraid. You still hold those qualities deep in your core and accessing them gets easier with practice. Use these positive features to inform your choices as a parent; don't let someone else do it for you. Partnering with your kids is too great a gift to give away to another's idea of your role. You own this moment - step into with your full self, not some shell of who you might be. Be the parent you want to be, the parent you already are at your core, beautiful self. What do you bring to the table?

Mantra: What's my best self?

Try this: Recall a time you felt full of possibility

Avoid: Getting lost and feeling unsure

Reconsider the Rule

Rules are placeholders for real decisions. They are quick and efficient and we give them way too much power. Using shorthand can be helpful but it can't replace actual discussion and examination of a situation. Trying to use an upright umbrella isn't helpful if the sun is coming from another direction or if it's too windy. Frequently shifting conditions require custom approaches, so don't put so much weight on a pre-determined answer. Try to zoom out and find the value you are trying to communicate. Put the emphasis on a direction rather than an outcome. A rule of "we don't hit" isn't helpful for someone who really needs to release a physical sensation. Keep everyone safe by offering a soft pillow to punch in another room until the feeling passes. Look for alternatives rather than whipping out an inflexible, unforgiving hard line. Problem resolution falls to you, not to a rule. Your responsibility is to think.

Mantra: What's the point here?

Try this: Name the desired value

Avoid: Being arbitrary

My Own Action Idea

Mantra:

Try this:

Avoid:

My Own Action Idea

Mantra:

Try this:

Avoid:

CONSIDERATIONS

Do you compare your childhood with your child's? Why or why not?

_____
_____
_____
_____
_____
_____
_____
_____

How are your experiences different?

_____
_____
_____
_____
_____
_____
_____
_____

What feelings do you carry as a result of your history?

_____
_____
_____
_____
_____
_____
_____
_____

Identify Accountability

CONSIDERATIONS

How do those feelings impact the way you parent?

_____
_____
_____
_____
_____
_____
_____
_____

In what ways were you given opportunities to learn from mistakes?

_____
_____
_____
_____
_____
_____
_____
_____

Can you remember what it was like to be a carefree kid? If not, imagine what it would have been like and describe it now.

_____
_____
_____
_____
_____
_____
_____

CONSIDERATIONS

What things would change if you just let your child be a child and not the cause of your happiness or sadness?

_____
_____
_____
_____
_____
_____
_____
_____

What rules or old ideas need to be re-examined?

_____
_____
_____
_____
_____
_____
_____
_____

In what areas can you let your child off the hook?

_____
_____
_____
_____
_____
_____
_____
_____

CONSIDERATIONS

Specifically what behaviors, requests, situations bother you?

_____
_____
_____
_____
_____
_____
_____
_____

What do you know about yourself, your thoughts, your experiences, your relationships that would explain why you are bothered?

_____
_____
_____
_____
_____
_____
_____
_____

How can you separate your reasons above from the actual behavior, request or situation?

_____
_____
_____
_____
_____
_____
_____

CONSIDERATIONS

Your child has two responsibilities: to learn and to grow at his or her own pace.

You, the parent, have two responsibilities: to gently support learning and growth; and to maintain appropriate thoughts and feelings.

List specific ways you both will fulfill these responsibilities.

Child can learn this	How Parent can support

CONSIDERATIONS

Why might this be challenging?

_____
_____
_____
_____
_____
_____
_____
_____

What positive actions can you take to move around these obstacles?

_____
_____
_____
_____
_____
_____
_____
_____

Tell yourself why it's important not to blame and punish your child but to help him or her as they learn through their mistakes.

_____
_____
_____
_____
_____
_____
_____

Step 4: Identify your Direction

How to Get a Peaceful, Workable Resolution

. . . .

What You Will Learn

° How to Use Feelings to Achieve Desired Goals

° How to Develop a Partnership that works

° How to Decide what to Do Next

° How to Open to your Child's Experience

° How to Stay in the Moment

. . . .

There may not be a "solution" every time. But there certainly will be an ending, a resolution. What will it be like? Let's open up to the possibility of this ending well.

We all have experience with things not going the way we want them to. Regret can be consuming and poison your ability to improve your problem-solving skills.

You can lead yourself to believe that the best way to fix something is to just end it as quickly as possible, usually by issuing commands like *Be quiet!*, sending someone to their room, threatening to leave or taking something away. Or worse, raising our hand to spank, slap or rinse mouths out with soap.

We can get stuck in those routines, those scripts and forget that there are other ways. You might get a short-term fix with those other methods but how effective are they really in the big picture? Is that the kind of conflict resolution you want your kids to learn? Is it important that you claim your authority and demand respect for your final say in the matter? Can you invite dynamic participation instead?

This Helps Accomplish

° Building a Trusting Relationship

° Security for Your Child

° Progress Towards Calmer Interactions

By taking a moment to envision how you want the situation to be handled, you open the door to that happening. Much the same way that a soccer ball goes in the direction of the follow-through, your result will follow the direction you set. If you point yourself in the direction of cooperation, you're more likely to get it. If you determine to yell and be angry, you'll get yelling and anger.

Once you begin to see alternative responses it gives hope and keeps you on the path. By giving a voice to what you want you can plot a way to make it happen. Ideas will flow and you can move with confidence and happiness instead of tension and dread.

This step is about slowing down and focusing on your child. How can you work together? How can you develop a partnership that reflects who he is and what he needs at this time in his life? You won't be able to use force always so isn't it better to not rely on it now? What you are building is a foundation that you will continue to tweak and grow as he does. At some point, he's going to be too big for you

Note: It may take years to see the fruits of your labor. Patience! Try to have both a short-term and a long-term vision here. Your child may not respond in the way you have worked towards this time. Go for the bigger picture of just being there calmly for them.

to pick up and put in the naughty corner. These are the years that you can use to develop your communication and understanding of each other so that you have a solid relationship in those later years. Learning how to negotiate, concede and empathize are critical life skills that you are imparting each time you discuss your differences or your child is having a difficult time.

You didn't have a child so you could argue with him or her. Parenting offers a unique opportunity to support and guide a life from the very beginning.

Effectively nourishing your child includes creating an enriching experience of being your child.

Enjoying your parenting experience comes when you release your expectations and open to the power of possibility. Developing an attitude of *I'm listening, so let's see what we can do about that* creates a place of loving team spirit. Knowing there are choices is so helpful! You aren't stuck and it's possible to hop outside of that endless loop. It doesn't have to end in tears. There are so many ways you can offer hope, help and your hand.

Our kids really want to believe they are not in this alone and that you are willing to hold them through it.

When I've been in conflict with my own child, this step has helped pull me back from the brink, more than anything. There was a time or two or a hundred that she wanted something I simply could not give. It was not a matter of me withholding her object of desire - I truly did not have the ability to get her what she wanted at that very moment. All offers to get it later were rejected. She was completely unreasonable because she wasn't old enough to reason yet.

It was so hard for me to stay calm after repeated attempts to help her understand. With her unrelenting reactions, my emotions spun rapidly to the dark side. I wanted to yell back at her, react with my own inner child's pain. I could see myself picking her up or dragging her to her room until she was no longer upset. I might have threatened her with not going to the park if she didn't stop.

All of those scenarios were rinsed away in a cleansing rain when I peered through the clouds long enough to see the sun. What was the best I could hope for? If I had a choice (and I did), what did I want at the end of this exchange? I could easily picture how I wanted it to end. I wanted to be cuddling with her, reassuring her that everything was okay, giving her peace and hope and love. The last thing I wanted was to hurt her. Picturing those two very different options saved me from regrettable actions and led to many sweet connections instead.

Remember, this isn't about using your authority to make things go your way.

Your goal here is to clear your head so you can prevent a downward spiral. If you think you can get what you want all the time, you are setting yourself up for disappointment, feeling like a failure and sabotaging the whole process. The purpose of this step is to head in a positive direction, increasing the chances that you can smooth things out amicably.

Let's explore some action ideas you can use immediately.

38

Offer a Hug

Sometimes something as simple as putting your arms around your child is enough to wash everything else away. (In his anger, he may push you away. Let that be okay. You have sent the message you are there if he wants to be held.) You can help your child feel respected by asking if he want the hug first. Notice how small he are, realize how much he is growing. You play a huge role in this development and as you hold him close to you it makes it difficult to be angry.

Mantra: When in doubt, give a hug.

Try this: Sit behind him/her and wrap your arms around so he/she can lean into you

Avoid: Isolation

Aim For Closer

What can you do to bridge the gap? Try to get as close to a "yes" as possible. Think of how you can find alternatives that will satisfy the need or desire. If the doll is too expensive, can you find it cheaper online or at a thrift store? Save up? Find another doll of the same size? Put it on the birthday list? Imagine you are connected by a fishing line and you are reeling them towards you as you work through this together.

Mantra: Bridge the gap.

Try this: Brainstorm ways to make it happen

Avoid: Not committing to helping

40

Connect

Tap into your maternal instincts and look at your whole child. You know them. Find a way in through a crack that shines their light. What do they enjoy? Can you use that as a way to get their attention, to take their mind off the trigger? If they like to run, challenge them to a race to the car. Make it fun! Humor? Exaggeration? Movement? This is a great chance for them to get to know you behind all that seriousness. You don't have to just be the large and in charge Mom. Let them see the person that you are. Share yourself with them and watch them open up as well. When you engage them on common ground, it's an experience they want to share and they relax into it.

Mantra: What does he/she like to do?

Try this: Play truth or dare

Avoid: Being too authoritarian

41

Focus On the Next Moment

Don't get overwhelmed or you can lose track of where you are and where you want to go. Keep the big picture in mind but focus on the baby steps that will get you there. What's the one step you can take that will draw her nearer? What's the one after that? If it breaks down, let that go and pay attention to your next step. Try something else until you get there. Remember: the next step may be simply riding it out without making it worse.

Mantra: What can I do next?

Try this: Don't look at the clock

Avoid: Getting ahead of yourself

Realize You Have a Choice

Your child was not born with a manual. Likewise there are no parenting books that contain absolute, universal rules. There are options. Methods. Advice. But it's all up to you. You get to decide what course you're going to take. Throw the rules out the window and go with the flow of what the moment is telling you. What does your child need? Proceed with loving-kindness.

Mantra: This is my chance to decide.

Try this: The nicest thing I can do is...

Avoid: Doing something that feels wrong to you

43

Release

There are times when nothing you do helps. Or so it seems. In those cases, the very best help you can give is to surrender. Don't throw in the towel or "give in." Simply realize that it's too big right now to be contained. Find a safe space and allow the tears, the release. Stop any physical harm but offer safe alternatives for these feelings to be let out. It can be very cathartic to move a body in response to the energy that is raging inside. Stay near with a grounded presence but don't force anything or speak. Release your expectations as your child releases her feelings. Eventually it will stop and a hug might be needed.

Mantra: Just let it go.

Try this: Imagine you are a mountain that can't be moved by this

Avoid: Bottling up big feelings

44

Worst/Best Scenario

Scan your feelings for what will feel the best/the worst. Will there be smiles or tears? Will you have regrets or joy? Will you be planning your next adventure or biding your time together? Will you be playing the video game together or will you be taking it away? Will you be comfortable with each other or trying to figure out how to break the ice? The more you can flesh out the details and feel the scenario, the easier it will be to know where you want to land and how to get there.

Mantra: How do I want this to end?

Try this: Use all of your senses to build your final scene

Avoid: Not having something to work towards

45

Make a List

Brainstorm. What are your options now? What are you looking to accomplish? What are some ways that you can make that happen? Remember that you always have more than two choices. There are the two extremes and many places in between. Let your mind wander over the range of possibilities and be open to suggestions. Maybe you just need some time to cool off or some focused time together or a game of hide and seek or a quiet drive around the lake. You don't have to be perfectly happy or extremely mad. Look at all of the other ways you can relate to each other.

Mantra: Where do we go from here?

Try this: "I don't want us to be mad at each other all day. What can we do to change this?"

Avoid: Not knowing your options

46

Give It Time

Don't rush it. Emotions can be big, scary things. Just as we get stuck there, so do our kids and they can't process as quickly as we can. Having a dose of patience while they get their balance and recover from the intensity and confusion of the situation goes far. Simply hold the space for them to move into a receptive mode. It will come, even if it's painful for you to watch or hear. Don't leave them alone, stay close. Keep offering your lap or your attention but be ready to wait a little bit longer. A good cry can be very cleansing when the child is supported and feels safe and loved. Can you create that environment while he processes his emotions?

Mantra: Just give her/him a little time.

Try this: Sit on the floor and wait

Avoid: "Just stop it!"

47

Alternatives

Forget your default response. Build on the options you already know you have. Can you be creative and try something new? Let go of the idea that you "have to" do what you first attempted. Be willing to delay or re-arrange your plans, ask someone to take your place, make it more fun and inviting. If the overall goal is warmth, see that sweat pants are a fine alternative to pajamas. It's always helpful to have lots of ideas in your toolkit as kids change and become more receptive to new ways. Look for ways that suit your child's personality and temperament.

Mantra: What if I try...?

Try this: "Let's go when you're finished with your game. I can wait."

Avoid: Getting stuck in a rut/insisting

Can You Take It Back?

When you are reviewing your options consider whether you want it to be on your record. Once you put it out there, you can't undo it. Carefully decide how much weight your actions hold and how far-reaching those effects can be. You are not just raising a child, but creating a legacy. The way you parent will be the model upon which your child will parent, too. What will he remember when he looks back on his youth? Were you kind? Did you react in anger? Did you punish often? What words did you use? Name calling, spanking, abuse and threats damage. Don't act in a way that you would want to take back. You can't.

Mantra: Am I sure I want to do this?

Try this: Don't do something you don't want to be accused of later

Avoid: Permanent harm

49

Apologize

Say you're sorry. Make sure you tell her that this has nothing to do with her and you love her. We make mistakes, plain and simple. It is honorable and the right thing to do to admit you were wrong and apologize. Ask if you can start over and really do start over.

Mantra: I love you and I am so sorry.

Try this: "You didn't deserve that and I was wrong."

Avoid: Leading your child to believe it's okay to be treated badly

50

Clean Slate

Give your child a fresh start. Just as you can't take back your actions, neither can your child. Give her an opportunity to begin again. Forgive and forget, let it go. Do you have to hold on to everything? How important is it really? Do you think that not wiping the slate clean is going to help her learn something more valuable than what you can show her through your forgiveness? If it's that big of a lesson, there will be another opportunity to learn it, perhaps when she is older and more ready for it. Give her a chance to try again by letting it slide.

Mantra: We need a clean slate.

Try this: "I'm going to forget this just happened."

Avoid: Carrying grudges and resentment, burdening your child

Re-Write the Story

We all have history that informs the way we parent; reasons that we struggle to handle things ideally. There may be a method that is so well-worn in your memory that it's automatic, even when you don't want it to be. You may have ideas about the way it will go because "that's the way it always goes." Change it. You don't have to settle for a way that you don't like or doesn't work. Blaze a new path for *your* family. Be inspired to take a risk and follow your own best idea instead of a familiar pattern. The ending is affected by your direct action and while it may take some time, it's worth it to write your own story. Your parents wrote theirs. This is your turn.

Mantra: It doesn't have to be this way.

Try this: Dream big

Avoid: Repeating history

52

Build Trust

Encourage your children by demonstrating that you are on their side. They shouldn't have to guess whether or not you will support them, help them, guide them. Be there, encourage them, give them so much confidence in you that they are willing to talk to you, be honest, and listen to what you have to say. Trust is a two way street: if you want it, you have to give it. Be willing to hear them, really hear them. Be open to their suggestions and take them. Be able to hand over some decisions to them, more and more all the time so they get to practice taking responsibility and grow in faith that you trust them. You have to mean it.

Mantra: How can I build trust?

Try this: Let your child decide

Avoid: Having too many rigid rules

53

Err on the Side of Love

Parenting can be scary. We don't want to make mistakes that jeopardize safety, health or happiness. We worry about getting them through the day but also impeding their futures. This fear and overwhelm can cause us to act in ways that we don't like but we hope are best; in ways that we regret and punish ourselves for later. Tough love falls into this category. Don't do that! Instead, look into your heart of hearts and feel that deep unique love that only you possess. It is strong and capable, and like an evening tide it can gently wash away any pointy debris. When in doubt, choose the action that is based in love and faith that everything is okay. It usually is but we can interfere by letting our fear take over the interaction.

Mantra: Love trumps fear.

Try this: Find a way to be safe

Avoid: Being harsh and unreasonable

54

Build Up

When your child is having a tough time, lift him back up. He may get stuck in negative feelings or thoughts, unable to see the light. From that place, he needs you to remind him of his worth. Tell him how wonderful he is. Remark on the good qualities, the unique traits that he brings to the world. Make it easy for him to bounce back because he sees the positive value of his participation. Your child has wonderful things to offer. Help him operate from those gifts by reminding him he has them. He may fail but you can show him his footing again.

Mantra: You are so good at...

Try this: Recall a good deed or accomplishment

Avoid: Letting him/her feel like a failure

My Own Action Idea

Mantra:

Try this:

Avoid:

My Own Action Idea

Mantra:

Try this:

Avoid:

CONSIDERATIONS

Imagine a situation you commonly find yourself in with your child. How does it usually unfold? Now, go back to the beginning and look forward: What is the one thing you can do to keep it together?

_____
_____
_____
_____
_____
_____
_____
_____

How do you want it to end?
What kind of relationship do you want? See how
you'll be relating emotionally and physically. Will you have a
resolution? An agreement? A plan of action?

_____
_____
_____
_____
_____
_____
_____
_____
_____
_____
_____
_____
_____
_____
_____
_____
_____

CONSIDERATIONS

What happened to get you to your desired ending? Did you pick her up and hold her? Ask questions? Make an offer? Where did you begin?

_____

_____

_____

_____

_____

_____

_____

_____

When has this worked for you before?

_____

_____

_____

_____

_____

_____

_____

Do you have other techniques or advice that have worked in the past?

_____

_____

_____

_____

_____

_____

_____

_____

CONSIDERATIONS

How can you free yourself from distractions in the moment?

_____
_____
_____
_____
_____
_____
_____
_____

Do you have a phrase or word that reminds you of what matters?

_____
_____
_____
_____
_____
_____
_____
_____

What does your desired destination feel like?

_____
_____
_____
_____
_____
_____
_____
_____

CONSIDERATIONS

Identify Your Direction

What did you uncover in previous steps that could help you here?

_____
_____
_____
_____
_____
_____
_____
_____

What can you accept in the short-term to achieve your long-term vision? How does this help your child?

_____
_____
_____
_____
_____
_____
_____
_____

How can you let go of the need to have the perfect resolution?

_____
_____
_____
_____
_____
_____
_____
_____

CONSIDERATIONS

How do you want your child to feel/believe about you as her parent?

_____
_____
_____
_____
_____
_____
_____
_____
_____
_____
_____
_____
_____
_____

How can you show your child kindness, love and understanding?

_____
_____
_____
_____
_____
_____
_____
_____
_____
_____
_____
_____
_____
_____
_____

Step 5: Conduct a Review

How to Process Your Experience

• •

What You Will Learn

° How to Create a Short-Cut to Solving Future Issues

° How to Feel Better About Your Experience

° How to Release and Integrate Your Feelings

° How to Move On

• •

This is exhausting work. It's also important work. Let's process and preserve what you've learned for your own self-care and to reinforce your toolkit.

There is a massive amount of energy spent when you are engaged with emotions, even more so if you have physical encounters with your kids.

They might swing at you or throw things, writhe on the floor, wiggle in your arms.

Feelings can take on the same characteristics and you may be left empty, spent.

Or maybe you feel tight, clenched, primed for a fight. Scattered, confused, walking on eggshells? These are not good conditions under which to live so give yourself some time and space to let it go.

Often we know just what we need to relax. A hot bath, a good book, some wine, chocolate. Just time to take a shower and brush our hair in silence? Oh, yes. Absolutely take care of yourself in these expected ways. Ask for the help you need to make it happen. Then go deeper.

Anxiety and concern can be exacerbated by a feeling of hopelessness. Banish that by acknowledging the steps you are taking. Be aware of all that you now know, the ways you are changing, the small victories you've tasted. Every step of the journey is just as important as the sweet arrival. Even if you've taken one step ahead only to slide back two, let yourself release the experience and its impact on you.

This Helps Accomplish

° Opening for New Beginnings

° Building More Confidence for Everyone

° A Grounded and Aware Sense of Self

° A Reference Point

When you've made progress, breathe that in and let go of your worry that you wouldn't make it this far. Instead of shaming yourself for what you've done or didn't do, decide to do better next time.

Don't hold your overwhelm, fear, disappointment or other feelings to yourself. Share them and ask for help.

Let go of negativity. Create space for other feelings and ideas to move in.

Especially negativity towards your child. It's over. It happened. Move on.

How can you use what you've learned to empower yourself and prepare for the next moment? That doesn't mean expect a conflict or outburst. Do what you can to smooth the way to happiness, peace and possibility. If you've noticed a pattern that your child gets upset easily if he's hungry, keep a snack in your purse and offer it before he's hungry. If you know that you are triggered by your child asking for everything she sees in the grocery store, shop alone. Once my daughter revealed it was hard for her to see someone else buying something for themselves, I made sure she wasn't shopping with us unless she was able to get something, too. With time and maturity she is much better at handling this situation but in the meantime, I prevented upset by not setting her up for it.

I am an intense person. My thoughts, my feelings, my actions tend to be big and quick and I can hold onto them for a long time. After a powerful moment, I need to release it all or else I may spiral back down. Even if it's a positive experience, it needs to be processed. My best method is writing as I am able to connect deeply to my feelings through words. Scrawling and scribbling can feel like a re-birth for me and it makes it very easy to move on.

> The stories we tell ourselves become exaggerated when energy ramps up. Putting pen to paper settles the dust and clears the air, creating an opening to begin again.

Often I can't even remember what I was so upset about because I emptied it out. There is a lightness that arrives and I'm able to smile and laugh and accept the love that is coming my way. My daughter seemed to bounce back when we had been at odds and was ready to love me immediately. Accepting that gift was difficult until I learned to wash the negative experience from me the way she had. I couldn't believe I was worthy of receiving her forgiveness until I had forgiven myself. By writing I also could conclude that things weren't as bad as I thought they were, including my own behaviors.

Find what works for you so you can move on.

Let's explore some action ideas you can use immediately.

55

Write It Down

It's easy to forget the details of an interaction but they might be important or helpful. It's helpful to make some quick notes about how your interaction went from beginning to end. What were the triggers, what did you learn, what worked, what didn't, how did it end, how does everyone feel? With a series of these you can pinpoint common issues, find solid solutions and gain insight that you might not otherwise find. If you don't like to write, make lists, record a message on your phone, make a note on the calendar. Find some way to document what you are experiencing for later reference.

Mantra: Make some notes.

Try this: Have a dedicated journal

Avoid: Forgetting helpful details

56

Write a Letter

Express yourself to someone - yourself at a different age, your partner, your friend, even your child. It doesn't have to ever be sent and you may want to make an agreement with yourself before you begin so you know how safe you are to talk about anything you need to say. If you are feeling great, mail the letter to yourself as a reminder of your success. This is an opportunity to say what you might not want to say out loud, ever. You can vent, you can argue, you can just dump it all out onto the harm-free page. It's a safety zone that exists to accept that which you cannot carry, cannot hold and cannot function with happily. Writing is an amazing release. Once issues are out of mind and onto the paper you can be freer of their hold.

Mantra: Write it out.

Try this: Don't think, just scribble

Avoid: Trying to ignore your feelings

Cry

When your kids aren't around, just let it all out. Crying is one of the most cathartic and healing processes you can use. Give yourself permission to feel sadness. Give yourself permission to express it in a way that you can see and feel deeply. Each tear that drops carries concern, worry, fear, anger, upset, fatigue, doubt, effort. Let it go. You might need a nap afterwards but you will feel so much better when you process your feelings this way. Parents try so hard to put on a brave face that we forget that we have a range of emotions that serve very deep purposes. It's okay to let them surface.

Mantra: It's okay to cry.

Try this: Get in the shower and wash it away there

Avoid: Pretending you're fine

58

Make a Plan

Use what you've learned to further understand the characteristics of what is happening, plan prevention strategies and identify what helped. You can use this information to help identify what the causes may be and possible immediate solutions for the future. If you have trouble thinking on your feet, have some ideas ready to go. You can't control someone, but you can look for clues that might give insight into how you can help them. No one likes feeling out of sorts, no child enjoys acting out. It's your job to be there in whatever capacity they need, even if it's just quiet presence until they are ready to be comforted. What can you do to help when the need arises? What can you avoid (including places and senses)? How can you plan to manage your own responses? How can you set yourself and your child up for success?

Mantra: Next time I'm going to...

Try this: Write your own Action Ideas!

Avoid: Throwing away insight

Pray

Spiritual guidance helps us feel less alone. We can feel held, comforted, supported, guided and aided. Regardless of your spiritual beliefs, you likely have prayed in some form. Sought respite? Needed advice? Wanted to make a bargain? Surrender to a higher power and offer your troubles in exchange for compassion. Feel surrounded by all those who have gone before and found that in the end everything works its way out. You are safe and you will be okay. There are resources to help you if you ask for them.

Mantra: I need some help here, Universe/God/Goddess/Grandma.

Try this: "Remind me that it's okay."

Avoid: Feeling alone and helpless

60

Burn the Fear

Literally and in a safe environment. Use strips of paper to note your fears. Or use an entire journal. Whatever you need to release, write it out. Give a gentle, *thanks but you can go now,* and burn it. Light a match and do it over the sink. Or light a candle near a bowl of water. Or start a bonfire and toast marshmallows in the glowing embers. Feel the warmth created by the light. It replaces the empty, hollow feeling that fear creates. Watching it go up in smoke is a great visual reminder that your worry doesn't have power over you unless you allow it. It can disappear by your own hand in a flash.

Mantra: Burn, baby, burn.

Try this: "You can go now."

Avoid: Holding on

61

Say Yes

Create joy. Just say yes. Let the "no" go and invite the possibility that floats in when you grant a wish. How great does it feel when you make an offer and the person replies with an *okay, sure, why not?, yes!*? Give that gift to your son or daughter. There are solutions to your reasons for wanting to say no. Worried about a mess? Take it outside or to the tub. Don't want to "spoil" dinner? Eat your meal a little later or plan a smaller one. Concerned someone will get hurt? Get involved yourself, find a softer toy, put down a cushion, move to a safer location. How much can be solved by giving the gift of yes? Release your immediate dismissal and find a way to make your child's suggestion happen. It might be more fun and easier than you think.

Mantra: Yes!

Try this: Become a participant

Avoid: Being an obstacle to get around

Say You Are Sorry

Everyone makes mistakes and there should be no shame in that. Model the most gracious behavior by admitting when you are wrong and saying that you are genuinely sorry. By taking responsibility, you are developing trust, creating credibility, showing that you are human, too, and that it's acceptable to admit it. If your child feels afraid to admit wrongdoing because he's going to get into trouble, will he come to you when he needs you? Help this along by being an example of humility and strength. Our kids feel it when we mess up and if we don't own that, who will they think is at fault? Don't saddle them with blame and don't expect them to take responsibility for your actions. Apologize to them and tell them that you will try to not make that mistake again. They will accept it if you are sincere.

Mantra: I need to make this right.

Try this: "I'm going to try harder."

Avoid: Letting your child feel badly for your loss of control

63

Start Over

Once the moment has passed, let it go. Belaboring a point or gossiping about it doesn't help move you farther away from the situation. What you need is to leave it where it belongs: in the past. You have this moment in front of you to begin again. Try not to carry over expectations that "it will always be this way" or "she's just like that." Give her another chance, give yourself another chance. You may need to start over a hundred times but that's better than condemning everyone to staying in the same place. If you want to move forward, you need to be willing to forget what might have just happened and pick back up where you left off. You may need to throw the whole book out and buy a fresh one with no underlined passages. Make note of what happens when you do.

Mantra: It's over and done with.

Try this: Erase the tape of "here we go again."

Avoid: Creating a trigger for yourself

64

Follow Through

If you say you'll do something, do it. I'm not a big proponent of being consistent because too much is always in flux and you can get trapped in something that no longer works. However, when it comes to promises or commitments you've made to your kids as part of partnership, it's important to follow through. You'll erode the trust you've gained if you back out of the deal. Will they negotiate with you again if you don't deliver on your word? Make a plan for how you will deliver.

Mantra: I said I would.

Try this: Put it on your calendar

Avoid: Breaking promises and eroding the trust you've gained

65

Go To Your Room

You might be needing some space. If you are feeling on the edge, leave before you explode. Put yourself in a safe place where you can be alone and calm down. Don't compromise this interaction and/or cause physical harm. Maybe you aren't on the verge of snapping but need some quiet time to release the energy of an exchange. Our adrenaline gets pumped up and can continue to bounce around inside unless we give it a chance to dissipate. You'll feel better faster if you take a few moments to close the door and breathe in calm and exhale everything else. Centering yourself is easier if you don't have someone tugging on you or asking for something. Ideally you can learn to do it anywhere, but sometimes it's best done privately. Give yourself some time alone to let the moment pass, get your feet back under you.

Mantra: I need some space.

Try this: Do your favorite yoga pose

Avoid: Exploding

66

Give Yourself Credit

You're doing the work. Rome wasn't built in a day and the Coliseum is still crumbling. It can take years to tear down systems and behaviors that have been in practice for so long, embedded in our memories, experienced all around us. Establishing a new normal is a process that requires commitment, consideration and courage. Take some time to recognize your effort and be honest about what you are working towards. Every time you make a different choice, you are changing the future. Each hug you deliver instead of a tongue-lashing is a positive move. When you take the time to act instead of react, you are putting another stepping stone in the pathway of communication and cooperation. It may at times feel like one step forward and two steps back, but keep going. You are doing this and it only gets better.

Mantra: I'm making progress.

Try this: Stack up the good times

Avoid: Giving up

My Own Action Idea

Mantra:

Try this:

Avoid:

My Own Action Idea

Mantra:

Try this:

Avoid:

CONSIDERATIONS

What do you need as a person? As a parent?

_____
_____
_____
_____
_____
_____
_____
_____

Take responsibility for providing that to yourself. How can you get it?

_____
_____
_____
_____
_____
_____
_____
_____

What does your child need?

_____
_____
_____
_____
_____
_____
_____
_____
_____

CONSIDERATIONS

How can you help?

_____
_____
_____
_____
_____
_____
_____

How can you work together?

_____
_____
_____
_____
_____
_____
_____

Do you get stuck in bad feelings and grudges, or can you give everyone, including yourself, another chance? How?

_____
_____
_____
_____
_____
_____
_____

CONSIDERATIONS

How does your child move on and do you help with that process? If so, how?

_____
_____
_____
_____
_____
_____
_____
_____

How do you feel after you have reacted in a less-than-desirable manner? How do those feelings affect other aspects of your life?

_____
_____
_____
_____
_____
_____
_____
_____

What do you enjoy in terms of relaxing? Is it physical or creative?

_____
_____
_____
_____
_____
_____
_____
_____

CONSIDERATIONS

Do you have the help you need to be the parent you want to be? If not, where can you get it?

_____
_____
_____
_____
_____
_____
_____
_____

Do you have the help you need to process your experience? If not, where can you get it?

_____
_____
_____
_____
_____
_____
_____
_____

List some ways that you would like to process your experience. What will help you empty your feelings and cultivate a refreshed spirit?

_____
_____
_____
_____
_____
_____

CONSIDERATIONS

What have you learned that can be used as a prevention strategy?
List as many as possible.

This   will help prevent   This

Quick Start

How can you set everyone up for success?

_____

_____

_____

_____

_____

_____

_____

_____

List your favorite action ideas for each step.

Stop before you Start:

Identify the Problem:

Identify Accountability:

Identify your Direction:

Conduct a Review:

Appendix: Lighten Up

Not everything is a big deep need begging to be filled. A little levity can go a long way, always. Try some of these ideas:

- relax   • pillow fight   • paint or play with clay together
- play with water   • take a bath   • water balloons   • swim
- move your body: dance, spin, swing, ride bikes, jump off things
- buy ice cream • throw eggs   • make nasty kitchen potions
- feed: belly, heart, brain, limbs that need to move   • play I Spy
- get creative   • move furniture, put on a disco ball and dance
- think outside of the box   • pick flowers   • climb trees
- look for alternatives   • run crazy races in the hallway   • wrestle
- tell a story or make one together taking turns adding a word
- talk in a weird voice   • sock wars   • make faces at each other
- pull out a game or puzzle   • play "would you rather" • bake a cake
- play with your pet   • cut up a magazine   • create a collage
- talk a walk   • watch old family movies   • run through sprinklers
- play dress-up • have a fashion show • sidewalk chalk
- put on a favorite video/comedy/tv show   • make popcorn
- let them give you a makeover   • have a talent show   • make mudpies
- have a food fight outside   • hold them upside down   • face paint
- get in the car and go for a drive   • play music in background
- bubbles   • use dramatic voices to complain about silly things
- paint in the bathtub have a scavenger hunt   • feed birds/ducks
- draw on windows with dry-erase markers   • "what's your favorite...?"
- make play dough or slime   • sing   • make sock puppets
- create a pinterest board together   • jump on trampoline
- have a three-legged race • create an obstacle course

Notes

About the Author

Flo Gascon is mother to two beautiful girls who provide endless inspiration to parent fully and with intention. Since the birth of her first child in 2001, her full-time experience has been in the acts of mothering that foster connection, confidence and communication. She knows how challenging it can be to not lose the way as a parent so she offers her learning experiences for the benefit of other families. She counsels through writing, conferences and online programs.

The best year yet begins anew each day. Alongside romping with her family on San Diego, California's sandy beaches and wrangling reproducing sticky notes, Flo takes photos, drinks tea and makes dreamy plans as she asks, "what is the best that could happen?". You can follow her at www.flogascon.com

Made in the USA
San Bernardino, CA
22 March 2019